# ELEVENTH TOE

ESSENTIAL POETS SERIES 104

Guernica Editions Inc. acknowledges the support of
The Canada Council for the Arts.
Guernica Editions Inc. acknowledges the support of the Ontario Arts Council.
Guernica Editions Inc. acknowledges the financial support of the Government
of Canada through the Book Publishing Industry Development Program
(BPIDP).

# JULIE ROORDA

# ELEVENTH TOE

*Julie Roorda*
*Sept. 9, 2001*

**GUERNICA**
TORONTO•BUFFALO•LANCASTER (U.K.)
2001

The author would like to thank Doug, Nancy, Dan, and Jackie Roorda, Ian Worling, Halli Villegas, Bruce Meyer, Austin Clarke, and the editorial board of *Pagitica*.

Copyright © 2001, by Julie Roorda and Guernica Editions Inc.
All rights reserved. The use of any part of this publication, reproduced, transmitted in any form or by any means, electronic, mechanical, photocopying, recording or otherwise stored in a retrieval system, without the prior consent of the publisher is an infringement of the copyright law.

Antonio D'Alfonso, editor
Guernica Editions Inc.
P.O. Box 117, Station P, Toronto (ON), Canada M5S 2S6
2250 Military Road, Tonawanda, N.Y. 14150-6000 U.S.A.
Gazelle, Falcon House, Queen Square, Lancaster LA1 1RN U.K.

Typeset by Selina.
Printed in Canada.
First edition.

Legal Deposit – First Quarter
National Library of Canada
Library of Congress Catalog Card Number: 2001086699

National Library of Canada Cataloguing in Publication Data
Roorda, Julie
Eleventh toe
(Essential poets series ; 104)
ISBN 1-55071-129-6
I. Title. II. Series.
PS8585.O683E54  2001   811'.6   C2001-900188-6
PR9199.3.R5865E54   2001

# Contents

Eggs 7
My Grandmother's Wedding Dress 9
The Myth of Her Bunions 11
Fire Thrower 13
Church Basements 14
Purdah 18
There's a Glitch to Every Truth 19
The Evolution of Thanks 20
Dundas Street Bridge 25
May Day 26
Peaches 28
On Grenadier Pond, in a Blizzard 30
They Will Find 31
Evidence 32
Skimpy Love 34
When You Go 35
Wishbone 36
Pessimist at an Air Show 38
Between My Teeth 39
Rod and Staff 41
Photosynthesis 42
Spring Cleaning: Dust to Dust 43
The Big Bang 45
Transcend 46
Designated Navigator 47
Kindergarten Perspective 50
The Edge of Night 51
Alien Abduction 53
Bodies of Water 54
Love and Augury 55
Eleventh Toe 58
Sleepwalking 60

# Eggs

I was astounded that my mother
could prick holes in the poles of an egg,
like a brain surgeon removing a plug
of bone from a skull,
and not shatter it completely,
then blow in one end till the insides
streamed clearly from the other.

She entrusted me with one,
and interfered only to warn:
"Don't burst your ear drums,
don't breathe in."

With pots of primary colours,
a lit candle to drip wax,
I created a globe,
ice caps around the poles,
blobs of green
surrounded by wider blobs of blue,
continents slightly rearranged.

I kept it long past Easter.

I liked to hold it in my hand
and toy with thoughts of its fragility,
imagine civilizations blooming,
tiny dots in fields of green,
then falling in
along the cracks,

if I chose
to squeeze too hard,
and sometimes I peered
through its poles at a mirror
looking for the reflection
of my own dark eye.

# My Grandmother's Wedding Dress

She snuggled against her sister,
imagined her fiancé's warmth,
and turned a defiant shoulder
to the radio droning
through the bedroom wall,
a draught, chilly words:
*The Queen Wilhelmina has fled.*

She fought to swim downward,
deeper into sweet dreams
where water in her ears would buffer
the thunk of Nazi boots in the kitchen,
the sounds of strangers swallowing
a familiar breakfast.

Her mother dragged her to the surface
with a touch on her arm,
fingers that smelled of fried potatoes,
voice alarming in its calm,
"Sh-shh, children,
stay in bed."
Then returned to her kitchen,
to the guests.

Her siblings huddled alert
to the dank air of their
northern mudflats
abandoned by the surf,
and she rose from her bed

to the window and the morning
on her world, yesterday's
new sprouting beets now
draped in a rippling black sheath
where they landed.

She sucked salty breath
through her teeth
and whispered,
"Silk!"

## The Myth of Her Bunions

My grandmother had legendary bunions,
a new knob or spur for each child she bore.
There were ten in all. "Twenty years on my feet
and not an hour without pain!" she'd claim
with pride from her place in the kitchen,
where the linoleum sagged with wear.

For me, at age four, rhyme was its own logic,
so I conjured up this horror: Grandmother
standing contorted by the stove, one foot up,
slicing swollen, fragrant bunions into a sizzling pan.
That, I understood, was why her feet hurt,
and why I could never stomach her soup.

When I was a teenager and slightly better informed,
I learned that her condition is hereditary,
and came to dread – instead of her soup –
those babyish and huge flat soft leather shoes
that moulded around the vegetable bulbousness
of her feet. They were deformed, distinctive, ugly.

Since she died, I've heard that bunions occur
where one steps unevenly along the ground
tilting disproportionately toward the inner edge.
The foot responds with armour to this hefty weight
of earth. If I choose to change my gait, that fate
of mythic bunions just might be avoided.

But what would my grandmother have done
had she known this? Taken a load off
and learned to walk again? I suspect
she would have stuck with her sideshow status:
a topsy-turvied Atlas,
juggling a globe on her bulging toes.

## Fire Thrower

Lightning hit a nerve in our house,
blowing out bulbs and the radio,
setting off the smoke detector
although nothing was ablaze.

My niece, who was visiting, screamed
and her parents ran to comfort her
with an innocuous, scientific explanation:
"The air is clapping for the fireworks."

But the toddler narrowed her eyes
suspiciously – the tyranny
of their five senses
that denied her understanding!

My parents used to assure me too:
when the air began to quake
and the night fell over day, they'd say,
"God is rearranging his furniture."

And I'd think how inconsiderate
God was to alarm my tiny heart
which detected invisible smoke,
only to be told there was no fire.

# Church Basements

I must once have been
fond of church basements.

Something stopped me at the green
"Rummage Sale" banner over the entrance
to St. Vincent de Paul.
                        It was not
the strange man in an antique
three-piece suit, who gulped a shot
from a goldish flask and tweaked
an imaginary hat to the steeple cross

before he nodded and muttered, "After you."
He followed me. I followed pink arrows,
fish pointing down the stairs and into
a low hall where the old mould smell rose
as seepingly as flood waters,
nose-filling.
                      There were four rows
of plank tables edged with splinters
and piled with clothes, forlorn
as forgotten laundry. Several sensibly-shoed
women waged a winless war for order,
folding and folding. Others stood
on guard for petty thieves.

"Has it occurred to you," the man said,
"almost all of these
clothes belonged to someone dead?"

He rummaged along across from me,
moving as I moved. "It's true,
people die with full closets." He
held out a cracked satin dress, once blue.
"Pure vintage, some of this."

I touched it, but the figure I imagined
could not have filled that voluptuous dress.
Instead I thought of the old shriveled woman
I viewed by accident when I was eight.

We'd entered the wrong room at a funeral home,
my mother and I, and only caught our mistake
beside the coffin, the body, shrunken as a gnome,
was not our dearly departed neighbour Mr. Hedy.

"If it's not old," the man said with a smile,
"well, there might have been a tragedy."
The spandex bicycle shorts I'd pulled from the pile
felt dusty, suddenly with asphalt grit.

I dropped them and, feeling the air
too thick in my lungs, stepped away to sit
on a sliver-infested chair
vacated briefly by the wall.

Its unrelenting plywood back,
the mind-jarring squawk of metal
legs against tile flooring cracked
open a memory of old Sundays
that sounded and smelled the same,

in a different church basement.
                                      Days
of simple confidence proclaimed
by popsicle-stick crosses, abundantly glued
and decorated and paraded for proud parents

that we might always keep in mind – should
I die before I wake – death and its consequence
if one fails to fashion crosses in church basements.

He stood before me with two date squares
in cupcake papers, purchased at his expense
from the requisite bake-sale table at which pairs
of ladies took turns, each selling her own tray
of identical pastries.
                                  He tapped mine with his,
a kind of toast. "To life! What can you say?
It all comes round to this:
ladies with date squares have the last word."

I bit into the sandy-sweet certainty
and found it cloying, stuffy, a bird
caught in my throat. He
swallowed his whole and grinned.

He left me and carried his musty armful
to the woman at the cash box who shunned
the flashy calculator for paper and pencil.

I heard him chuckle, "The wages of sin,"
as he opened his wallet. I fled.

The petty thief catchers' suspicion,
rose with alarm to see me leave empty handed.

I defied the arrows and emerged outside
cheered to find it raining and tried
to catch the drops,

                to wash away the toxic residues
of tragic moulding clothes and outworn shoes.

# Purdah

I've seen you
shocking as a giant crow
standing between mini-skirts
in line for the bank machine

only your eyes
and your hands weighing
ripe mangoes at the fruit stand,
testing firm flesh beneath your thumbs

your dark voluminous folds
draw the brunt of June
reflecting off plastic
the turquoise stroller
pushing your infant boy home.

The fruit you put back
squirts sticky juice
along my bare arms
the hot breeze, the sun
kiss the backs of my knees.

# There's a Glitch to Every Truth

The open grave is lined with astroturf.
His adult children gather
a step off the mud
and sing the hymns he depends on
to conjure the psalmy landscape
of his heaven.

They pray
he'll be re-united with his wife
and she will recognize him

that the heaven she evoked will be the same one,
she will not have left already
with that first young soldier husband
buried under a white cross
in the Netherlands.

The coffin hovers on ropes above the hole
– when the crowd is gone, they'll lower him in –
his children circle, chant the apostles' creed,
*and life everlasting, amen.*

## The Evolution of Thanks

Each Thanksgiving, before grace,
Mother admonishes us to wait behind our chairs
while Father takes a photograph

of the splendour on the table.
She'll have it to compare during next year's
preparation, and measure plenty's progress

in the march of vegetables and sauces.
Before she cooks, I remove all these photos
from an aging unmarked album

and tack this evolution of thanks
on the bulletin board kept in the kitchen
exactly for this purpose.

I poke each push pin through the same hole
in the white edging, without enlarging the wound,
and nudge it tightly to the cork.

In the earliest, there's a Bunnykins' plate,
mine, the first time I sat at the big table,
the first holiday I remember.

The rest ate from royal-blue
rimmed wedding china, a set still complete and intact
– not so poor Bunnykins.

We fought over the turkey skins
browned to near transparence
and a lick of salt.

One of the losers always cried
at the thought of a full year
before the next chance to win the favour.

The cone of whipped potatoes is yellow
in the older photos, as if the butter
has already been mixed and is not waiting to erupt

from the crater at its peak, lava and ash
that will bury hunger in a flash if you
don't leave room for other things.

Like two kinds of stuffing, oatmeal
and sausage, one in each end of the bird.
And one brother at each end of the table,

too far apart to use their Daisy Chain
stainless-steel forks for sticks and stones,
limited to name-calling.

Or brown sugar burnished carrots
cut roundwise, like the candlelight curling
along Anna's freckled hairline,

and her lips bitten red in protest
at being given water for wine
in her chunky crystal goblet

unless she could swallow
her Brussels sprouts, which she couldn't,
even when she was eighteen.

The lozenge of cranberry sauce
in a lead crystal dish, a ruby circled by diamonds,
till we cut it with a spoon,

reminds me of how Mother's engagement ring
etched lines in the insides of water glasses
when she washed the dishes.

Heirloom mahogany backs of the dining set
were retrieved just in time from Great Auntie Penny
who cracked and bought a pot of ashes at a yard sale.

She set it at the head of the table, in the one chair
that had arms, and an extra layer of cushion.
She did not object to giving us the furniture,

for our larger, younger family of six,
it made perfect sense. "I have no need of it," said she
who had never married,

"now that I'm a widow," and she cradled the crock
to her cheek and filled my pockets
with figurines from decades of Red Rose Tea.

When Raymond seemed about to speak,
Father reached out and touched his wrist
just as he might pass the buns

with floury tops that transfer fingerprints
to the deep red napkin in my lap
which catches things dropped, like a secret.

One year, there are red-eyed paprika specks on the corn,
a new dish prepared by Richard's fiancée,
that nobody liked, except Richard

who ate it all, then got sick before dessert.
Chocolate toffee meringue cake,
"Anna's favourite," Mother always said,

even when Anna no longer came for Thanksgiving.
She began many days ahead of the event.
Baked three fluffy meringues,

let them sit for one day, then assembled
the layers with chocolate and cream
and left it again to settle.

She prayed it would not list
on its way to the table – if it did
she would say, "Don't remember this,"

and shift the sinking side of the ship
away from the camera.
Meringues are unpredictable.

Unlike cauliflower cooked to translucent
thin-milk blue, as pale as Raymond
after his life went down the bathroom sink

in a wash of salty warm water.
He liked salt, used to cover
every item on his plate, heaving

the silver saltshaker Mother polished
three times a year, though we only used it once.
We gave up trying to stop him.

This year, there are only three blue-rimmed plates
on the table. The spread is more bountiful,
the turkey bigger than ever.

Mother rests finally in silence.
Father sets up the tripod and centres the table
perfectly in his viewfinder.

I stand behind my chair, think of how we've all grown.
"Step back," Father says,
"your knuckles are showing."

## Dundas Street Bridge

I was crossing the Dundas Street bridge
at an alchemical moment of zero
that slicked the gritty concrete below
my feet and I nearly slid over the edge.

I latched to the guardrail while the roar
of heavy streetcars shook the road
and the six o'clock Go-train ferried its load
of commuters to their bedrooms in Aurora.

The riders were immune to the needles of twilight
shooting pink dye through veins of the old
papery skin of snow. And just as the cold
conjures invisible breath to sight,

the half-light luminized the flux beneath
the surface of steady brick warehouses,
colour of dried blood, a flow rousing
new buds of rust on the remaining teeth

of broken trucks and machinery in a fenced
lot. They bloomed while I watched;
the growth of hibernation hatched
in that moment between now and the present.

## May Day

We stopped at a restaurant for a drink.
The first of May, and we simply felt lucky
to be alive on that auspicious evening,
caressed by the hypnotically warm
air. In conspiracy, the handsome waiter
seated us at a table beside the open window.

The table linen was pristine. The window
faced the busy street where we could drink
in the cosmopolitan sights until the waiter
returned with wine and his lucky
green eyes. He drawled in seductive warm
tones, "You're in for a perfect evening."

An aria floated out through the evening
din, harmonic, until a man approached the window
spouting gravelly throat sounds and a cloying warm
smell. He'd clearly had too much to drink.
He slurred, "Ladies, yer gonna get lucky
tonight," and glanced around for the waiter.

He fumbled in his pockets before the waiter
returned, producing a perfume labeled *Evening
Stars.* He sprayed an acrid poof. "For you lucky
ladies, five bucks." He stumbled against the window.
The bump jostled the table and toppled my drink.
Red wine on my white skirt, bloody and warm.

"Shorry," he leaned so close, I felt his warm
stinking breath on my face. Our waiter
snagged him roughly by the collar. "Drink
this!" the waiter spat and, heedless of the evening
traffic, shoved the man away from that window
which separated us, the safe and the lucky,

from the stunned, limping man who was only lucky
to be alive. The waiter with his green eyes and warm
smile shooed shocked onlookers from the window,
people staring at me, as if I had coaxed the waiter
on. The man staggered away through the evening
crowd, looking for his next drink.

We felt a little less lucky to be sitting in the window
where the warm air set the red stain on our evening,
and the handsome waiter returned with a fresh drink.

# Peaches

"Peaches are over," the grocer said.
He thrust his broom into the whirligig
of dried leaves which cycled in the corner
of his fruit stand that always caught the wind.

I bought them anyway, despite the shriveled skin
and grey thickness of fur – they might have been
preparing for winter. What a pity to be
a peach and such a late bloomer.

I sliced them and peeled away the caustic fuzz.
It used to raise livid rashes on the whites
of my wrists, especially in those late summer weeks
I spent picking peaches, before school resumed.

Those were sticky days, perched on tippy ladders,
and always reaching up. I could not stop
the juice of the occasional rotten fruit
from draining all the way to my armpits.

The boys got the better jobs
driving the cut-open station wagons.
They ferried full bushels of the peaches I picked
through the orchard to the sorting stations.

"Never trust a hot cranky woman in a car,"
is what the farmer who employed us
always said. We girls were sent
on foot to the heavy-laden trees.

Jokes, though never addressed to me, rose
with the steams of chemical-ridden dew. They evaporated
in the heat against my body, which, like the almost ripe
peaches, was really just one big itch.

Unscratchable. September peaches
dry as thumbs of woolen mittens,
taste of pesticide, cling to an overlarge stone.
I should have known. Peaches are over.

## On Grenadier Pond, in a Blizzard

no stirred reflections in dark water
no shadows of sharp sun
no salty borders of bare flesh

no, my skin is so muted
by layers of cold and wool
that I cannot even tell
where I begin

the wind has muffled the scenery
with deconstructing dots of grey
there is no way to step back
I am a fuzzy series of specks
in this Impressionist scape
where there are no outlines

if things were summer clear
I could not stand here suspended
where there is no difference
between water and sky

it's as if I haven't
been born

# They Will Find

Microscopic skin cells
beneath my fingernails

one long, light brown hair
in your sock drawer.

# Evidence

Yesterday you found one of my hairs
lodged between your teeth
like unwaxed dental floss.
I wondered whether these pieces
retain any sense of me.

They say hair and nails continue
to grow when a body dies –
so they might still be alive
when cut or plucked or filed.

And if they are alive and there is a link
I might just transfer consciousness
to that bit that has sallied forth
to the unknown crevice
between your gums and your plaque
like a Mars land rover

and it might twang back
messages in Morse code
saying, "There is life here!"

But like all good spies,
they can be used against me.
Mould those toenails into a doll
and you could control me,
swallow that hair
and I'll never leave.

Or they might of their own accord
take on our forms
like thousands of shattered broom bits
commanded by a sorcerer's apprentice,
and sense who we are
even when we don't.

They'll stand on end
or dig into skin
to see our future

and when our hair and our nails
have continued to grow
for a time after death
– only then will we know
why they stop.

# Skimpy Love

The thongs are narrow
on your bikini-love
holding all the crucial bits,
as you see them, in line,
while the rest
erodes with exposure.

Why can't your arms
be enormous as a tent?
A blanket held open by the car
when a thunderstorm
cuts frigid slices in the heat
and I run soaking
from a beach
to be warm, encompassed
drinking thick cocoa.

Your hands stay somewhere
between hold and reach,
and I have nothing
to dry my face

for you are skim milk,
wet dog-smelling,
thin and good for me.

# When You Go

Take a strand of my hair,
a small Romantic show of attachment,
even though you are leaving.
I'll take a lock of yours
and braid it for a brooch
like Victorian women who passed long days
plucking hairs all around
wresting into wreaths, elaborate,
harmonious as if all of one head.

Give me one from your crown
so I can imagine it still
bound to the top of your soul,
an astral cord stretching to me,
and you'll feel the tug.
Leave me several for my tears.
How easily strands snap when wet.
Even if I could number every hair on your head,
I could not hold you here.

## Wishbone

I've got a wishbone
caught in my windpipe
lodged near my larynx,
I can't speak.

I must have been
impulsive as a headless chicken
to have swallowed
this possibility whole

and whoever discovered
the premonstrative properties
of fowl bones must have been
someone as unlucky in love

as me, belatedly
discerning she'd always
come up with the short side
of the V.

Now it is tight as a bow string
poised, arrow pointing
downward, aimed at my heart,
tensed in anticipation

of this act of divination
which cannot occur till I cough
it up, and the bone,
dry of gristle and grease

becomes graspable – pull
till those legs are open.
There'll be one wish
and one bone broken.

# Pessimist at an Air Show

When you hear spitting engines start the show
you think of disasters that might transpire:
crashed planes swallowed in Lake Ontario,
spinning wings foiled by earth and turned to fire.
You imagine death – that mach force pressure
might snatch the pilot's consciousness, control
loosed to the elemental whims of air,
dangerous potential, to rise or fall.
Why do you automatically see
what lurks unemerged? What horrors might drop
when those children inhale with each volley
the thrill of a free-fall caught in a swoop?
They look up, and do not wait for the fall,
their lungs expand with danger's potential.

## Between My Teeth

If I could only get my teeth
around my loneliness
the way my cat arcs her jaw around the skull
of a vole and cracks it open!

I first associated teeth with loneliness
when I heard the story of Jonah
tossed overboard, swallowed whole
and imagined him peering out through a fence
of huge teeth, feeling terrified.
In fact, he was engulfed by the very live presence
of the whale that had rescued him,
when he was cast out of human company.

Then there was the tooth-lined pit
in the *Star Wars* movie
which digested its victims slowly,
over hundreds of years – several lifetimes
alone in an intestinal tract without end.
How did the devouring creature-pit
keep its victims alive for so long?

My cat consumed the whole body
of that vole. This morning
she caught a bird
and left for me
the bone-lattice work of its wings,
featherless and picked clean,
the machinery of flight laid bare.

When you sink your teeth
into my shoulder and wrap your limbs,
wet and heavy as sea-mammals
around my muscles, I think
nothing separates us like flesh.

# Rod and Staff

Soldiers in Vietnam used coathangers
to divine for landmines.

The same instinct seeks out death,
ulterior fire,

as a wellspring in the hands
of a water-witcher.

The upended pin I stepped on
sought life through layers of thick dead skin

which held tight, like good leather.
I needed pliers to pull it out.

The spot of blood a purple bead
on the sallow surface.

Pins in my path.

How many angels dancing on their heads.

# Photosynthesis

Unlike the full foliage which we get used to,
before the entire summer changes colour and falls –
>   the maple blossoms.
>   A mere intuition of leaves.

Then for five days, green rain.
The same five days for the whole city, as if on cue:
>   a certain angle of the moon,
>   an astral alignment we used to track.

It covers the ground with a kind of green
that is indefinite about its borders:
>   a knee-deep aura
>   above the layer of blossoms themselves.

Just a few weeks ago this glowing carpet waited.
Its disparate components unwoven:
>   muddy puddled water,
>   unsoaked sunlight,
>   thawing brown mulch.

>   Last year's leaves.

My mind gnaws on the memory of an equation
duly learned, then forgotten an hour after:

>   an inadequate explanation.

## Spring Cleaning: Dust to Dust

The living room carpet
possesses the same range of colours as the yard
this time of year:
> worm-brown ground,
>
> unyellow grass,
>
> pea-green of poltergeists that wait
in pre-leafed trees.
> It too craves lightening.

I sling it over the clothesline,
find a broom handle, unscrew it from the brush
and beat its wings.
> It deadens my swings
>
> with weighty force,
>
> its fibres still thick with the thunk of earth.
Chickadees fluster away
> from the airless explosions.

Dust is ninety-percent dead skin,
fragments of all the guests who transgressed
the living room this year.
> Microscopic minions
>
> that tug at my nose hairs,
>
> beg a burst of wind to scatter them
back to the elements.
> Spring is winter sneezing.

Each carpet ripple sheds another.
My mother's skin, white-gloved, fingering the shelves,
or my father's
>ever unremoved
>of over-polished shoes
>(who knows who he dragged along in the grooves
of his soles),
>the skins of strangers.

And old skins of me
outworn, each transfers the mood of its shedding
appropriately:
>tired flakes find damp ground,
>angry bits sun-bake,
>a startled chickadee ingests a mote
that rose up stir-crazy.
>Spring basks like a fresh snake.

# The Big Bang

The cosmic housewife
whacks her carpet with a broom,
then rides it away.

# Transcend

I thought I saw a footless woman
by the pond.
It was the fronds of an arching willow
that gave her form.
It was the wind of the shivering willow
that gave her airs above the ground.

Her hair was green
like a witch,
as indiscriminate about the season
as her sanity.

I offered her my own
green hair, a gift
to her irreverence
and never stood so close
as to transcendence, there
between the willow woman's stony shore
– stones to fill my pockets with –
and the water's wily current
offering
to take me out to lake.

## Designated Navigator

I don't know the back of my hand very well.
I've spent too much time examining
the map of my palm, hand turned upward,
a gesture even dogs understand.

This map has no scale to indicate
how many years equal a millimetre,
no arrow pointing north,
no topographical shading to show
if the longer lines represent
the scenic routes,
and whether the shorter,
though more direct,
will cause significant wear
on the transmission.

I was never good at reading maps anyway.
I couldn't coordinate the trip I traced
with what you were doing behind the wheel,
couldn't translate my intention to right and left,
couldn't choose.

Remember the short-cut through the Cascades,
how the car travailled on the incline, threatened
to dash out of bounds going down
and plunge through the clouds
that were below us.

We both thought the sulfury smell

was a natural phenomenon,
a dormant volcano, a portal to hell,
till we realized it moved with us,
and the car was burning.
We left it to cool,
walked the slope to a looking post,
a terrace above a gorge as steep
as an intake of breath,
the vein of white water obscured by mist
from the ridge of a damn,
condensing on the fat metal rails,
which looked shiftable,
a row of subway turnstiles
that would tick me off as I passed,
on my way down below.

It seemed a lesser risk to try the car again,
than to stay, cold and stranded
in the mountains,
so we got back in, continued,
consulted the map.

\*

When you reach a fork in your palm
how do you know which road to take,
the choice is fate –
but is fate the best choice?

If I were to turn my hand,
I'd view the solider side,
the side that conceals a card trick,

the thicker skin
that curls around a fist,

the side that will only begin
to reveal itself in advanced age
when the skin turns tight,
like a wet Kleenex over blue veins,
blue blood that never bleeds.

Dogs might cower away

and I'd see
the outline of bones beneath,
the girding of knuckles that seize
onto steering wheels,
or railings,
or ether.

Then you'd know me,
like the back of my hand.

## Kindergarten Perspective

I've been trying to remember
that pre-school state of mind that sees
the branches inside lollipop trees,
cradling a nest – because I know it's there,
home to far-flying birds, romantic Vs
darting among the yellow spikes of sun,
and, as if I'd been eye-level with the earth,
the green grass above the brown ground beneath.

So I asked my niece to colour on my walls
to reintroduce me to that mystery
of limbs sprouting directly from smiley
heads, flesh irridescent purple and aqua.

She did. She drew my house, and me inside,
then hid it all with swirls of deep blue sky.

# The Edge of Night

High above me,
a dark hump along a branch
like a boa constrictor
that has unhinged its jaw
to swallow a goat, still alive
and howling from the inside.

I find a flashlight,
and in its beam perceive
how the branch arches
toward its flimsy end,
where one screaming raccoon clings,
while another barks
and lurches threateningly toward it.
An invisible chattering chorus watches.

I imagine the thud,
the thick split corpse
on the patio in the morning,

or a survivor,
landing on its feet
to be a nestless misfit,
disoriented, wandering the streets,
an outcast rodent on the edge,

I shine my flashlight on the barker's face
as if to say, "You have a witness. Don't do this."

But it moves. The beam shines on to Sirius,
and the drama decrescendoes
to an end, no thud,
just the pattering
that might have been
applause.

## Alien Abduction

The plastic weave of the lawn chair presses
plaid patterns into the backs of my thighs.
The evening's first chill, a cold baby finger
touches my neck, and I know eyes

are peering from the eavestroughs, waiting
for the summer night transformation, clear
heat, molecule by molecule dusking
translucent, the air becomes a dark mirror

for scrying. They skitter along to a flimsy
branch (which would not hold their weight by day),
then descend, bulbous bodies irrationally
graceful. They'll pause in a precarious crook to play.

Their rattering rattering dialect of infiltrators,
foreign to the light, is exalted in this half-night
transit. Masked eyes rule the planet,
outside time and the square kitchen window light.

The scritching stops. They've landed, camouflaged
against the ground, their eyes surround and
mesmerize to stillness. A mosquito's hot pin
stinger draws a blood sample from my hand

while I cannot flinch. They are closing in.
Their long intelligent fingers graze the aluminum
bars of my chair. My hair stands on end.
I wait for the touch that will make me one of them.

## Bodies of Water

Think of a body of water:
not an ice-shot waterfall,
not a swan-embroidered pond,
not a lapping blue-dark lake.

Think instead of that icy leak
osmosing through your tired boots
at the bleak midwinter thaw,
that wince of realization
when your ramparts have been breached
and you have succumbed

to the same, slow, ferocious force
sloughing the pristine snowfall
(remember it? fluffy as newborn skin?)
to the sewers and into basements,
spreading sundry life-forms
that will remain
unsuspected in un-dry carpets.

I wonder if this is what it is like to die:
a sudden wince of realizing
one's ramparts have been breached
and the fluid soul is seeping
out to join
other bodies of water.

## Love and Augury

Did you know
you can determine
the date of your death?
Just tape a calendar
to a dartboard,
cover your eyes,
utter obeisance to fate,
and aim.

Do not ask her to name a year,
just a month and a day.
This way, you can mark your own
passing away, annually.

You can brand the day
with convention,
planting flowers on your grave

or with comfort,
feed yourself Jell-O and soup.

You can preserve your own memory,
or learn something new.

Fly to Mexico to cliff dive
for the sheer fear
of being and alive

or test the windows

in a high highrise.

Splash yourself
across tabloid headlines.

This is one date each year
to have everything done by,
to reorder priorities:

change the kitty-litter,
or quit your job?

There's more.
For you can also determine
the manner in which you will die:
just ride the streetcar,
and gauge how people react
to this occasion.

If everyone is speaking in tongues,
you'll die licked by flames.

If they are silent, but smile,
you'll be buried alive
on an anniversary some days
before this one.

If they are silent and frown,
you will certainly drown
in a Great Lake
and frigid water.

If they are all wearing red,
you'll transpire in bed
wrapped in limbs
of an illicit lover.

But if the moon is blue,
rest assured,
they will rue the day
they killed you.

It will be more festive
than New Year's, when midnight arrives
and you know, *you know*
you've at least one more

in which you won't starve
or be hit by a streetcar.

Understand, that you can
aim to celebrate
both the nights you know you won't die
and the days you know you might.

So come and stand beside me
on this day of our life or death,
accept the dart I give you.
Close your eyes.
Take a breath.

# Eleventh Toe

There is an extra toe on my left foot.
I believe she is my identical twin.

I have worried that I was so greedy
in the womb that I deprived her
of the attention she needed
to become more than a hidden limb.

And in return, she has denied me
the opportunity to squeeze into regular shoes.

I've tried, only to be disabled by her consciousness
surfacing in livid, bloody blisters:
"Consider that I am you,
that you are the superfluous digit."

It's true, we cover more ground together.
Bare in the summer we span a wider arc of earth,
so wide, we can feel her curve.
We would not have survived in Galileo's day.

We'd have been be-headed or be-toed,
depending on whose perspective we chose.

Sometimes I think I'd prefer hers where it is closed,
although stuffy, and eventually I'd be aching
to stick my neck out again, like she,
clamouring for air and a voice.

Now I worry, if I am less greedy
and pay her the attention she needs,
will she grow to be an alternate me?
Will I become her eleventh toe?

# Sleepwalking

Mom tells me this story frequently:
she found me that night
flailing over the rail of your crib
trying to climb in

with you, who were the baby,
though you seemed so much older to me,
as if I'd been sitting at your feet
for centuries.

I was still unconscious
when she lifted me down
and she had to keep turning me around
before I'd sleepwalk back to my bed.

In the morning, I remembered only
dreaming through my fingertips,
without vision, without voice,
just a brush of your soft face,

like a pilgrim grazing the worn paint
of a saint's cheek in an antique cathedral
where zealots have scraped away the eyes
to keep us from gazing on God.

Your eyes won't open again,
nor your mouth — you had never spoken.
But that touch lures me through centuries
of silence and darkness.

I am still sleepwalking toward your crib.

MEMBER OF THE SCABRINI GROUP

Quebec, Canada
2001